Birds of New Jersey

poems

Susan Rothbard

The Broadkill River Press
Milton, Delaware

Acknowledgments

Thank you to the editors of the following publications, in which these poems, or earlier versions of them, first appeared:

The Comstock Review: "Kitchen"
A Constellation of Kisses: "First Seating"
The Cortland Review: "The Marigolds" and "That New"
Dogwood: "Someone Else's Life"
The Literary Review: "Bitch" and "Feeding the Birds"
Nasty Women Poets: An Unapologetic Anthology of Subversive Verse: "Your Bitch"
The National Poetry Review: "Mythology"
Naugatuck River Review: "On the Corner of 18th and Park"
Pif Magazine: "PMS at 45" and "What You Own"
Poet Lore: "The Phlebotomist's Dream" and "Your Voice"
Spindrift: "Ways to Step into the World"
Tiferet: "Your View"
Twyckenham Notes: "Interruption" and "Prix Fixe"

"Mythology" was awarded the 2011 Finch Prize for Poetry. "That New" was chosen by Ted Kooser for his newsletter, *American Life in Poetry*. "Feeding the Birds" was featured on *Verse Daily*.

My deepest gratitude to the many outstanding teachers with whom I have worked. Special thanks to Renée Ashley, Jeanne Marie Beaumont, Robert Carnevale, Cat Doty, Maria Mazziotti Gillan, Peter Murphy, Madeline Tiger, Sara Vap, and Laura Winters for their inspiration, feedback, and generosity. I'm grateful to the Geraldine R. Dodge Foundation for scholarships to the Fine Arts Work Center and to the New Jersey State Council on the Arts for scholarships to Artist/Teacher Institute.

Many thanks to Ken Ronkowitz, Barbara Whitehill and Leon Alirangues, with me from the beginning; to Mary Florio and Svea Barrett, for their careful attention to my work; and to Alissa Pecora, for sharing the journey. To my workshop group at the 92nd Street Y, thank you for helping to make this book happen. I'm especially grateful to Malcolm Farley for his meticulous reading of every poem.

Much appreciation to Linda Blaskey, Coordinator of The Dogfish Head Poetry Prize, to Sam Calagione, CEO of Dogfish Head Craft Brewed Ales for sponsoring the contest, and to Jamie Brown of Broadkill River Press for all his help.

Sarah, Barry, and Jeff, thank you for being my biggest fans and inspiring so many poems, and Jeff, for loving even the mean ones.

Published by The Broadkill River Press, Milton, Delaware
broadkillriverpress.com

BIRDS OF NEW JERSEY

In memory of my parents,
Florence and Gerald Kaye,
and for
Jeff, Sarah, and Barry

Contents

III

I

Your Voice

Your voice will always sound the same, but when
you call and give your name to strangers
they won't know it's you the way your mother
does each Sunday when you dial her number,
ask her all the questions you have asked
her every Sunday: how's the weather, how's
her neck, the leaky roof, her dying friends.
And all the time you talk, you stand and stare
outside, more taken by the cardinals
that have returned to your backyard today,
her answers drowned by all that red. You count
them—eight, you think, though when they flit from branch
to feeder fast like that you can't be sure.
There's nothing sure about the birds, of course;
you know these eight might not be those you saw
last week. But still, you want to think they are,
they know your house, they've sent word that here's
a place, a home that's always full of seed
and they will always come and you will learn
their song and something in your voice will change.

Matryoshka

The only story she ever told me:
Her mother died when she was ten. I know

it by heart—the train ride to Alabama
while her mother lay in a New York hospital,

the relatives who talked in whispers,
the funeral she did not attend,

the train ride back to a silent father,
the lonely walk to school, the stepmother

whose first husband hanged himself, who fired
the housekeeper who was the closest thing

to a mother my mother had, the bench
in the park where she sat after school

eating chocolate-covered donuts, stuffing
them into her mouth, she was so hungry.

On the Corner of 18th and Park

We've just come from Paul and Jimmy's,
    where Paul and Jimmy's sons joke about who
        is younger—calling each other *Grandfather*—

and wait on the tables themselves. It reminds me
    of Ernest and Werner, the German restaurant
        on Main Street in Orange where my father

would take us for Sunday dinner—it felt more
    like someone else's kitchen than a restaurant.
        But it was torn down decades ago, and even

the Mexican restaurant that replaced it is gone.
    I couldn't tell you what's there now, just like
        I couldn't tell you what happened to Golden China

one town over, where no one thought it dull
    to order wonton soup, egg rolls, chicken chow mein
        and where the fortunes in the cookies didn't seem

like platitudes. Back then I believed in the future
    the way I now know that what's taken away
        is not always what's given. It's long past bedtime

and we still have the ride home in front of us—
    past the post office on Eighth Avenue that makes the idea
        of mail seem epic and through the Lincoln Tunnel

where you can know exactly when your body straddles
the line between New York and Jersey and shout,
I'm in two states at once! That's where I want to be

right now at 11:00 on a Saturday night,
leaving a restaurant that's been around for longer
than I have. On the cusp of something.

If You Don't Have a Dog

you can leave for the city at 6 AM,
and maybe you won't make it home
until the next morning when,

if it's September, you might see
a yellow bus stop to load up
children wearing packs on their backs,

and you'll worry how someone
on a motorcycle can stop
if he comes around a corner too fast.

The thought leaves a bad taste in your mouth,
reminds you how tired you are,
how last night the book kept slipping

from your hands as you tried to stay awake
waiting up for your son who, you worried,
would not walk through the door. (Instead

the phone will ring and you'll hear
a low voice saying something you don't
want to hear.) This is how fear worms itself

into your life no matter what you do—
except when you're with the dog,
who's happy to bring the same orange ball

to your feet in any kind of weather.
This should be enough. Think
of all the people who don't have dogs,

how they ride the train home,
coming back late, the cars ablaze
with fluorescence, the tunnel leading out

of the station so dark that all they see
when they turn to the windows
are their own faces staring back.

Bitch

When my son tells me he hopes I die,
last week's curse—which at the time

seemed the worst thing you could say
to your mother—fades from my mind

along with all the other things he's said
that I know he doesn't mean. All I see

is the look on his face when he hears
his wish has come true and he'll never

be able to take it back, the taste still in his mouth
and my voice in his head. I move in close,

hoping the words I say in return feel as hot
to him as they do to me. I rant, my face so near

his I could lean in for a kiss. I don't.
Something ugly sits at the back of my throat

and he sees it, and I want him to see it.
Tonight I want to be mean, want to find

his softest spot and make it hurt.
I don't want to be his mother—the hardest

thought I've ever had. But if I'd seen some sign—
no, not tears—but say his eyes had grown wide,

I would have left us both alive.

Arctic

after watching Sue Aikens on Life Below Zero

Because she cannot ever know just when
she is about to fall or if the snow

will be too deep or whether bears will come
from east or west or that the sledge will make

it up the hill, she keeps a gun beside
her at all times. Beer, bullets all she needs

and a ptarmigan or two to cook along with
couscous and dried fruit. So clear, the snow

untouched for miles, except by sun and now
and then her skis which glide and shush and yes,

she has to brake at times but not too hard. It's white
and white wherever she turns and *all so nervous*,

hearing sounds and sounds beneath the sounds.
Whatever waits outside her door just *wants to eat*,

same as she—the birds that stare as she draws near
do not dissemble—as if they know she'll take inside

what she has caught to braise it. And praise it too.

Just When You Start to Feel at Home

you have to leave. You arrive in Paris,
say, your body still pulled by New York's
gravity. You board a bus and tour the city—
the Champs Élysées, the Seine, the long wall
of the Louvre—and you're as out of place
as the naked thinker in Rodin's garden should be.
The next day you walk, begin to feel the ground.
You chirp, *À tout à l'heure* to the concierge
as you leave the hotel, but still, it's someone else's
mother tongue—for all you know the men across
from you on the Metro are plotting to pick your pocket.
It's not until you've seen the attractions—Notre Dame,
the Eiffel Tower, Mona Lisa's smile—that you let
yourself stop at a café. Now it's the waiter
you watch, his shiny pate, pencil behind his ear,
apron double-tied. You wonder if the little girl
singing to herself in the corner is his, why she's not
at home or school. You see a couple embrace
in the middle of the street. A man on a bicycle
loses his cap. This is where you'll return
tomorrow and the next day. By your last visit,
the waiter will know your name and how you like
your coffee. These are the things you'll remember
when you return home and your husband holds you close.
You'll feel his fragile heartbeat, and it will scare you.

First Seating

Flu season, so we're not kissing
unless you count the smooches we wave
to each other as we sit down to eat.
We'll be out before the second seating
comes in with glitter eyes and muscled arms
that reach across the table to hold hands
and order tapas to share as they dip their forks
from one dish to the other, from one mouth
to the other, their evening beginning
as I tuck myself into bed, flossed and moisturized.

By the time they've paid their bill,
I'll have embarked on my tossed journey,
flanneled in a bed that knows
the contours of my body as well as I do.
I should begrudge them their passion,
but I've my own circadian rhythm that knows
the leftovers I brought home may not be as full
of promise as lithe tongues dancing together,
but I've eaten this meal once already,
and I know it will be good tomorrow.

Prix Fixe

Sometimes a rock at the edge of the woods
is just a rock at the edge of the woods.

And so what if the understory's leaves resemble
hearts but two have grown over the rock

so that from the angle of my seat
at this farm-to-table restaurant they look like eyes?

Now the rock is poor Yorick's skull.
And the small boulder a few feet away: a ghost.

How do you feel about movies
where nothing much happens?

The scallops sound divine, bathed in a roasted pepper
coulis, but isn't it creepy how the rocks are watching us?

I would like a more permanent solution
to this wobbly table than a folded matchbook.

In the meantime, I will order sparkling water,
which will make you wonder if you've ever really known me.

Florida Oranges

Some years we'd get two crates the same week,
one from my parents, one from his, arriving
at the front door, each fruit nestled in its own
plastic cradle. So many we didn't know

where to store them. They soon filled up the crisper
drawers, so we stuffed them into any space
we could find—on top of a tub of margarine,
between bottles of beer on the lower shelf.

By the time we were through, the refrigerator
blazed with orange, and every time
we opened the door, always the chance
one would slip and the others would follow

like disobedient children, roll off their shelves
and drop helter-skelter onto the floor.
So many the gifts became a nuisance, like
the phone calls on Sundays asking us to visit.

Years later, we open the refrigerator door to our
own empty spaces, remember our haste to finish
the oranges, break them apart or squeeze them
into juice, get rid of them before they turned bad.

Feeding the Birds

I wanted them to come. Wanted cardinals,
jays, a goldfinch—that yellow most of all.

I bought binoculars, *Birds of New Jersey*,
learned to recognize mourning doves,

the black spots they shared, how they got
their name. My husband began to look

out the window each morning, shouted for me
when they came, bought a birdbath because

he'd learned that birds get thirsty. Our children
laughed at us as they raced out of the house,

but I liked all that learning. Then I learned
about grackles. I told myself I didn't mind them;

their iridescent blue heads were beautiful.
I didn't know they would take over, scare

the other birds away, that I'd admit
they were ugly, buy seed they won't eat.

Now the empty suet feeder sways like a hanged
man on the branch where the grackles

once perched, and I watch from the window.
I could not choose my children this way.

Kitchen

Because my fingers are smaller, I'm the one
who minces the garlic. He chops the onions
because they make me cry. His job, to sauté
the broccoli rabe, mine to make the salad.
I set the table, he grills the lamb. I heat
the water for the pasta while he cuts the bread.
Sometimes we stand together over a pot,
inhale cumin and peppers, eggplant and basil,
our heads together as if we are in love.
When we sit down to eat, we praise our work.
Here we have no doubt. We open a bottle
of wine and toast each other, forgetting
the fight about our son's curfew or whose
fault it was that the dog peed in the house.
And when our daughter calls from her matchbox
apartment and says she's searing tuna with a red
wine reduction, we can hear her boyfriend
dicing tomatoes in the background.
We can taste her joy across the river.

The Woman Who Combs Her Hair

The woman who combs her hair is not her mother
though her father insists that is her name.
She shuts her eyes, pretends to be in another

world, where girls who bed on cinders
sleep and dream and wake to dreams,
not this woman who combs her hair. *Mother*

tastes like ashes or feathers—they smother
(pillow, noose, pill) just the same
when she shuts her eyes (not pretending). Another

tug, and she is back in front of the mirror,
steeled against hands trying to tame,
comb through the knots her mother

left her (this and a sun-bleached picture).
Her father says she should not complain,
so she shuts her eyes, pretends to be some other

girl, smiles at the woman she is not to bother,
then hears the teeth hiss, stake their claim:
The woman who combs your hair is not your mother.
Her eyes close, cannot pretend to be another's.

Genuine

I want the bird-cries in the eaves of the mall garage
to be real, the way a child wants to believe in the tooth fairy
even after he's seen his mother slip into his room.

All those years of compassion—wasted
now that someone's told me they're recordings.
I've lost half a metaphor—the birds meant something—

though I never knew what each time I went to buy
a new sweater, pair of boots, or, best of all, a handbag
with lots of zippered pockets. (I'm all talk—

not a thing I could or would do about the birds).
Face it: nothing's as real as we want it to be.
The birds' screams mock me now—like someone

I know is calling my name, but no one I know is here.
I squinch my eyes. *Fool me once* . . . I lock my car. Twice.
But then I take the escalator down to the first floor

where I can touch the *genuine leather*. And oh,
how good it feels to pull the zippers back and forth,
their teeth always knowing exactly where to go.

February 15

Dozens of dozens of roses swaddled
in cellophane line the windows of Trader Joe's.
I've come to buy eggs, bananas, a bottle
of seltzer, though I've thrown in more:
pretzels, Gouda, mix for a cake
I may never make. It's winter—we live
from meal to meal, from fire to fire.
What pleasure we take is our solace
for all this cold, all this snow.
But today, at five, the sky is still blue
as the cashier offers me roses for free
and I walk to my car not minding the cold
so much. What a wonder it is to see shoppers
like me with cellophane poking from the tops
of their bags. We all want something for nothing,
we're all bringing home roses. I imagine tonight
across the county: roses, roses, opening, opening.

The Man Who Would Not Stop Cooking

Even after the freezer was full—three
quarts of lentil soup spiced with Andouille
sausage, leftover turkey chili, beef
carbonnade, all stored in tubs from the deli

and labeled with dates—even after hunger
was out of the question, he got up at six
on Sunday, was first in the market where
he'd fill his cart: everything fresh, no mixes

or even dried herbs in a jar. The kitchen,
which always smelled of curry or sage,
came alive with the clatter of knives,
the countertops covered with discarded bay

leaves, the juice of crushed tomatoes, his joy
as he lifted the cover of a pot to the melding:
always stew or soup or ragout—nothing broiled
or baked in its juices alone. Each evening

a new mélange, and we did not ask why
or say *Enough*. We filled our plates, cut bread
to soak the sauce, made noises while we ate.
We were a choir, our song a tribute to what is good.

Mythology

The albino deer comes every day now,
suckles on the bird feeder like a baby
nursing as we stand behind the window
inventing its life, which, we all agree,
is not a good life, must be a lonely
life, because the other deer with their smooth
brown flanks move in a ballet only
they know, and our strange thing does not move
with them, and even the dog knows it's not the same,
doesn't bark, as if to say there is nothing worse
than loneliness and what kind of game
would it be to chase what has already been cursed,
and now we're closing the shutters, and now
we're turning away from the window.

II

Someone Else's Life

It occurs to you like one of those bolts of lightning
in a comic book: there's been a huge mistake.
It's the woman who lives next door who should be
pulling into your garage. Somewhere along the line
paperwork got lost. Someone is responsible:
the coach of the team you didn't make in seventh grade.
Your mother's stepmother. The matchmaker in Kiev.
It could go that far back. Or merely to the day
you were born, when you came out gasping and a strip
of plastic was strapped around your wrist. You were claimed,
named, but the manacle was meant for someone else.
The face in the mirror seems, not unfriendly, but strange.
Why, when your son calls, don't you recognize his voice?
How did you dream yourself behind this desk?

The Phlebotomist's Dream

She is drifting down a river in a narrow boat
just big enough to hold her. She floats
toward the mouth of the river, one of many rivers,

infinite rivers, and she, with only a fist

for an oar, must lie still so the boat won't give her
up to the belly of the river. She knows
that the water is cold and bottomless; the fish bloat
and burp bubbles. Trees line the bank, light shivers

through branches, and she with her only fist

cannot steer toward shore, cannot even see through the mist
rising from the water. Somewhere ahead, the river is bleeding
into a lake or sea. This is the marrow and grist
of it: the boat on its blind path in the midst
of something familiar and strange, forever and fleeting.

Ambiguity's Invitation

When she asks you to join her on a trip,
(as usual she's vague), you say yes. Your last
one, it rained, and something made you sick,
maybe the water. So *somewhere* seems just
the right place to go. Packing, for a change,
is not traumatic—she insists you'll find
all you need when you get there. You arrange
to meet at the edge of the river behind
the house where you grew up. You don't expect
to see your mother, are even more surprised
that your father's holding her hand. When you left
them last, he'd been laughing at the way she cried.
They watch you get on a raft without oars
as something shifts on the opposite shore.

Here in New Jersey

She yells *Happy Birthday* across the world, excited
because it's my birthday where she is though not yet
here. It's one AM in Pompeii and my daughter

has spent the day walking its salvage:
frescoes, aqueducts, plaster casts of people, animals.
She calls now from a crowded square nearby.

I can barely hear her over the noise in the background.
I'm picturing a scene out of *Casablanca*,
only it's me and her, not Bogart and Bergman.

We stand by the plane, the wind whips our hair, she
has one foot on the step and shouts in a tongue
I can't understand. The propeller picks up speed

and she climbs away. It's 79 A.D.
Vesuvius boils like a pot on a too-hot stove,
and it's getting harder to hear her over the din.

She is hours ahead. Tomorrow sprawls
in front of her. There is no way I can catch up,
no matter where on this world we might be.

No Ticket

We were slow to figure out it was the roof
even after rain came in through the bedroom
ceiling. We'd wanted a fast food, grab-and-go
life, folding chairs and collapsible table, no
ticket bought ahead of time. But the house
had come with wall-to-wall carpet and mouse
droppings in the kitchen cabinets, mirrored
walls and sparkle-speckled linoleum floors.
We redecorated, exterminated,
had kids, made the house bigger, planted
shrubs, watched the water bills grow. Weeded,
replanted, saved for tuition, the much needed
vacation—suitcases, itinerary.
Oh, how we'd planned to be extraordinary.

To Ahab's Wife

Do you think about the years between you
and your husband when you stand on the walk
perched at the top of your house? Does the view—
roiling whitecaps and hawks' talons seizing

their prey—please you? Do you breathe deep
the salty air, hold it inside your lungs, feel
it catch like nicotine? Can you say the word,
relief, admit the joy of sailing without a captained

ship? At last, unmanned, you can pack your bags
and move inland. Leave behind the spyglass.
No need for a note or forwarding address.
Can you hear the wind chimes calling your name?

Your Bitch

After Ada Limón

I'm learning new ways to be a bitch. There are, of course, the old ways: There's how I correct adults who confuse *fewer* and *less*, and if I weren't such a bitch, I'd explain it here. And there's the bitch I can be when I'm driving alone, changing lanes. There's also the bitch I can be when I'm driving with you, and we get lost. There's the night before a trip bitch who hates to pack. There's insomnia bitch. There's 5:30 on Monday morning bitch and 9:00 at night laundry still in the basket bitch. There's rejection letter bitch and we can't afford it bitch and why can't we afford it bitch. There's silent treatment bitch and behind your back bitch, hot bitch and cold bitch too. There's the bitch who needs a drink and the one who's had too many. Then there's the bitch when you've had too many and I have to drive you home. It's teacher mother sister daughter best friend bitch. It's the bitch who tells the truth and it's also the one who lies. It's the bitch who won't stop barking. It's the bitch who's learning to bite.

What You Own

How much easier to live alone,
unfettered by people, surrounded by things
you choose. What you need is what you own.

Get rid of plants, whatever dies, and yes, the phone
book goes. How good it feels to lose the ring.
How much easier. To live alone,

though, takes courage, a nod to what you know
about yourself, which, you fear, is nothing.
You choose. What you need is what you own

up to wanting, and if you have to ask someone
else, you'll never know when to leave, what to bring.
How much easier to live alone

if no one's left behind when you're gone,
it's true. But still, it's *you* who clings.
You choose what you need. Is what you own

now enough? Then why not get it done
already? Or else admit this song you sing
is easier, and live with it. Alone,
you choose what you need, what's your own.

Exit Row

When the stewardess asks if I'm ready
to help in case of an emergency,
I say, *Yes,* of course, because I'm getting
extra leg room, which I hadn't foreseen
when booking the flight. I feel lucky
until I read the card that lists all the things
I might have to do if an engine quits
or a fire starts, and now I see the wings
for what they are: metal, too heavy to fly,
for sure, and I think of my husband
ten rows back, how I don't want to die
with my hand held by a stranger's hand,
but it's too late to say, *No, not ready at all;*
I look out the window: everything's so small.

En Vacances

There was that time we drove to Montreal
and pretended my name was Isabelle,
carried that secret to the gallery
where we bought a painting
of a goofy-looking couple,
kind of like us, grinning in bed.
Later, we sat at the dinner table,
a candle flickering between us.
When the waiter came, you asked,
Isabelle, what would you like?
just so we could hear the name again,
so that *he* could hear it,
as if that would make a difference,
and it did: I was Isabelle,
someone who would never say
the horrible things I said
on the way home when we got lost,
someone who was happy
to let you order for her.

The Marigolds

The marigolds still quarrel in the bed
we made beside the house last spring. With fall
near gone and winter on its way, we're ready
to be done with marigolds. We quarrel. The bed
they shared with parsley, basil, thyme has bred
another batch where none should stand at all.
Marigolds? *Still* quarreling? The bed
we made should hide, not house, such spring in fall.

Pinching Petunias

I grasp below the tiny cup
with its green pod inside
that once tricked me
into thinking it was the seed
of a new flower.
Not easy
to pull out such green.
And hard, also,
to clip the furled stillborn,
its skin, elderly-translucent.
Every morning, new blooms
and always some that droop.
Small help to know the difference
between the impostor
and the little bud
that reaches up its hand.

Perennials

Even though the pear trees are in bloom
and the goldfinches have returned

and the forecast is finally getting better,
the dog, with his lopsided grin

and tail that wags at the sound of my voice,
is beginning to limp when he climbs the stairs.

Even though last May, the beds were filled
with impatiens, petunias, marigolds,

now there's not a trace of them.
The crocuses and hyacinths planted in the fall

won't bring them back, and though
I thought the surprise of purple and yellow

would cheer me, today I'm reminded
that someone's always left behind to miss

whatever's gone. I think of them next spring,
rising to greet who knows what kind of weather.

Inheritance

Of all the things—pots and pans, pearls,
perfume, photos, even a baby grand piano
circa 1900—it was the pincushion
she prized most, that cloth tomato plump
and red as the day it was bought. Perfect
but for the needles with their tails of pink,
yellow, blue, and white thread used to piece
together, still there amid the spools and patches,
summer camp name tapes, buttons, safety pins:
a lifetime of notions for mending packed
into a satin-covered basket. Poultice
to the wound, magic fruit. Reminder of a past
that never was but still lets her pretend—
something to salvage, some thing to repair.

Smaller

Sometimes when I feel lost (I'm feeling lost),
I take a vacation from myself, leave
my body in its seat, spine straight, legs crossed,
while the rest of me (most of me) deceives
the world, rises like a runaway balloon
into the sky where I float over towns,
where every house is my house, and soon
every mother will wrap her arms around
me, a counterpane for my loneliness.
All this time, I'm getting smaller and smaller,
and the farther I let myself drift, the less
I can make out below, until it's all
mountain ranges, valleys, the sea—a map.
Slowly, I begin to trace my way back.

I Try to Explain

When the doctor tells me I should swim, I say,
    I can't do that, so he tells me to wear a life jacket,
        and then I try to explain that I *know* how to swim,

it's just all the—and here I use my hands
    like I always do when I can't explain something
        I'm trying to explain—waving them in circles

by the sides of my head as if I'm conjuring spirits,
    which is what it feels like when I try to explain
        something I know will sound wrong (like now)

but is the truth: it's the hair, the makeup, the chlorine;
    it's the drive, the startling water, what the babies
        in Family Swim have left behind. It's dressing

in a locker room filled with strangers. But I don't get past
    It's the . . . and he has no idea what I'm talking about,
        so I just drop my hands to my sides and nod, though

I have no intention of ever setting foot in a pool
    because how can I know that I'll welcome the rush
        of humid air when I open the door, that even though

there's a glass window, I'll never feel like anyone
    is watching, that the water will be warm and the lifeguard
        will always tell me to have a nice day as I leave, and I'll

believe he means it? How can I know that this is where
    I'll learn to love kicking hard and running out of breath,
        where I'll reach with my arms as if I can grab water?

The Sound

I love that you hear trains before you see them,
how they shush at first, then holler so loud,

the conductor loud too as he calls out
and you rush for the doors, pray they'll stay

open, and when they do, you feel like he's held
them just for you. You're going somewhere *now*

and it's *new*, as fresh as his blue cap that sits
in place no matter how hard the wind blows.

The train moves slowly at first, then picks up
speed, and when you cross the space between cars,

you hold on tight, see the rails below,
but you don't mind that you sway and bump

against steel doors—the sound carries you
into the next car. Even when you're not

getting on, it's enough to hear the sloppy
clanking, metal grating, like your mother

looking for a pot beneath the stove
when you were young. *Home*, it calls. *Home*.

Tenderness

Late September, we're eating breakfast,
I'm late for work again, don't hear the birds'
relentless cawing until my husband,
steam from his coffee shadowing his face,
says it's early for birds to be migrating.
I know he means he's sad that summer's
over, and I love that he's noticed. But no,
I tell him, they're not leaving yet.
They're just holding a meeting to plan
the trip. It's a big undertaking, which is why
they gather this morning behind our house.
They make noise like senators in a cavernous room,
decide who will fly together, who at the apex,
who at the tails. No one wants to be left behind.

The New Neighbors

At first we hated them for being new—
siding, windows, evergreens, their youth—
while our porch crumbled and the ash trees died.
When they invited us to their barbecue
and sat us with their parents, we hated
them even more. Their children too: the bikes

and scooters that littered the lawn, the school
bus making us late. But then the four-year-old
boy rang our bell, asked to play ball with our dog,
who waited for him at the window each day,

so we let them stay.

Ways to Step into the World

It is hot, and I have chosen to watch
            not the whales or the ocean which goes on
                        forever, but the painters clustered

in the shade, heads bent toward canvas.
            If you didn't know they were there,
                        you might mistake the flashes of color

for a bird's wing, or a tangled kite.
            One artist sees the scene in a wash
                        of pale greens, blues, browns. Next to her,

another idea of blue melds with orange.
            One man includes the detail of a broken
                        pier; the painter to his left lifts us to sky.

But I am most taken by the woman
            who has tucked herself in the shade so deeply
                        I think she is hiding. She paints a beach plum—

the fruit on her canvas magnifies the one
            on the tree. The other painters have made
                        the world small. She has made it so large.

III

Your View

It's still a surprise to see the moon
on a clear night even though you know
it belongs right where it is
above the evergreen you planted
when you first moved in, just to the left
of the birdfeeder you bought last summer
when you were trying to be like a woman
you admire who has a birdfeeder,
though you never expected you'd trudge
through snow to feed the birds which you fear
you've fooled into thinking it's okay
to stay through winter, and now you feel
this weight each afternoon when you come home
just before dark and the seed is gone,
and it's only after you've filled the tube
that you can take off your coat and read the mail.
Your devotion surprises you every day.
This is the view from the kitchen sink
where you scrub at the bottom of a pot
that won't let go of its stain, which is why
you draw in your breath when you see the moon,
even though it will always be the same moon.

PMS at 45

An excuse for everything from murder
to spontaneous weeping, it comes

with circadian precision. In her
younger days, she didn't mind so much. Numbed

by the reminder of what she could make,
she felt ripe, poised on the edge of something big.

But lately, the animal within shakes
the bars, picks at the lock, tries to dig

its way out. She will never be pregnant
again, so what is the point? Let it go.

At night, when something clamors in her chest,
let it be her heart, not this bird trapped in its nest.

Scars

Some of them you remember well: the fall
down the stairs when you were six, the thud, dull

as your shoulder struck the basement door,
or how swiftly the blood flowed when glass tore

into the soft flesh of your foot. You were ten then
but still can trace the story's line—again

your mother's voice is far away, unheeding.
And still today, you call and call, cleaving

to an idea of mother you've chased all these years.
But she's too swift, won't be caught, and now appears

beneath your skin where doctors probe and grasp
and tear. Anesthesia's a lover's name; it doesn't last,

and when you wake, the pain returns. Part of you is gone.

Fun Day

Anyone walking by must have thought
we were rude to be laughing so hard
as our mother lay dying, a bag beneath the bed

collecting urine while one above dripped morphine
into her arm, the three of us taking turns lying
on the other bed. When one sister said, *Remember*

Fun Day? we all did—how we drove along
the backroads of Georgia, lovebugs splattering
against the windshield as we made our way

to the factory where our father was king
and we were princesses, *adorable* and *beautiful*
according to the women who ladled soup

in the cafeteria and the men who ran the machines
that made the cans he sold. But on Fun Day
no one worked. There were rings to toss,

cotton candy to eat, we wore matching dresses
and Mary Janes, and our father, resplendent in coat
and tie, mother laughing in her linen dress, never once

said, *Stop bickering!* Soon enough we'd be sweaty
and sticky during the car ride back to our hotel,
the unluckiest stuck in the middle seat.

But we didn't talk about that part as we sat next to
the cart the social worker had wheeled in—teeming
with cookies, fruit, soda—anything we wanted.

Whither Thou Goest
          — Ruth 1:16

I tell her she looks wonderful, but Ruth
says, *We don't talk about the pain*, and though
I want to say I know how she feels, the truth
is, I don't. No matter how much my body hurts (oh
yes, and every day), her ninety years entitle her to claims
I should not make. She limps out of the salon
where we've met after so many years, the same
smile and tilt of her head I remember from when
I was young. I want to find out how she can ask
about my husband and children as if she cares,
how she *can* care. I want to be better at masking
my grief (already, yes) for all the pain I've yet to bear.
I look at her, namesake for one with a history
of pain (yet history's darling). I want her story.

Anniversary

Your marriage would look like an EKG
if you charted how long it took to choose
a card, a conclusion you reach as you stand
in front of the Hallmark display.

Haven't you given each of these before?
The one that jokes about sex or praises
his wise choice? How tired you are of the line
about opposites attracting.

Some years, it's easy, a two-minute stop,
but today, you'd rather shop for a bathing suit.
It's been thirty minutes, you're still undecided,
and the only cards left are blank inside.

Introduction to Quantum Theory

The climber who found Mallory's body on Mt. Everest
75 years after he disappeared couldn't tell if he was on his way
toward or back from the summit. He died before my mother
was born but was found after I had my two children,
which makes me think of Schrödinger's cat, both alive

and dead until someone looks at it, which isn't
the same moment as the moment it died, if it died,
which is to say, our dog's eyes were open before the vet
inserted the needle, and they were open after, too,
which is to say, I couldn't tell the moment he died.

Rappel comes from the French, *rappeller*, to recall,
which is to say that getting down from the top of a mountain
can be harder than going up, as Mallory must have known,
climbing *because it was there*—until he wasn't, which is to say
you can never know exactly when the hard work ends.

She's a fighter, the nurses said of my mother as she lay
in the hospital bed ten days after we were told it would be
a matter of *a few days*. My sister said she wouldn't have wanted
anyone to see her like that, gray roots, chipped nail polish.
She, who *put on her face* every day even if no one would see her.

Naming the Symptoms

Sometimes it's easy: the gash on your hand,
the wheeze in your chest, the rash on your cheek,
they point to a root, to a cure. They speak
for themselves. It's the ones you don't understand
that make you squirm in the waiting room
where the space next to *other* on the form
you've been given is far too small—where to start?
You'd like to use a metaphor—quarter moon
when you're touched, stain that won't go away,
hot breath on your neck, sound of a light
bulb just before it dies. Isn't this how we might
tell a lover what we want before we're able to say
Touch me here, no there, no there—?
You take your time with your height, your weight,
the place you were born and of course, the date,
but when you look up, you feel the nurse stare—
you're taking too long, it's time to go in,
take off your clothes, put on a gown,
breathe in, breathe out, open your mouth.
Say it: you want to feel like a woman again.

In the Middle of the Night

At three AM I thrash at the sheets, kick
them off, waking you with, *I'm so hot*,
and, once again, you lace your arms
around me, say, *I've always thought so*,
and we laugh. Sweaty as I am, I press back
into the soft it's taken us 30 years to find,
like these sheets washed so many times
we can almost see through them.
What comfort here in our quiet house
in the middle of winter, middle
of the night, to feel the thrumming
of each other's laughter
as if our bodies are one body.
Last week you said if you died now,
no one would say you were so young,
and I agreed, not to be mean,
but because it's true for me too.
I feel like we're boarding
a plane: unfathomable that we will survive,
unfathomable that we won't.
And there's this emptiness
every new moon when I lie in bed
feeling the heat spread like a blush,
as if I've said something wrong,
which I have, and more than once.
But now your fingers graze my eyelids
as if you can charm me to sleep.
Remember that time we saw
an old couple holding hands
and envied them?

Prognosis

What I hate about March is the tease,
not the roar, not the snow but the jonquil
(the polyp), the trick of the clock springing

forward until the phone rings and it's bad
news—what else could it be at this hour
of yellowing light and ridiculous promise?

We had them over for dinner, good friends in good
health, and they talked about travel, their trip
to Australia, as we sat in the kitchen, ate

cheesecake she'd made from her grandmother's
recipe, brought to our house still in its tin.
When she leaned toward her husband to feed him

a bite, I wanted her life. I liked hearing
them hum about the cake's texture, planning
how much better it would be the next time.

Not for Nothing

Not for nothing rain *can* fall for 40 days,
the un-collared dog knows his way back home,
and alright will never be all right. Say
it another way and the stranger on the phone
just might get what you mean, though it's hard
to know what you mean these days, five months
later and your dead mother's clothes still hanging
in her closet. Not for nothing, but—what?
When you pressed your nose into her coats last
week, it was for nothing. And when you wear
her earrings, you see your face in the glass.
A fact: your mother died, and it took nearly
five months for you to cry. No one's bothered
except you. Not for nothing, she was your mother.

Interruption

You will never look back on this and laugh,
though why is it so different from when you see
your mother naked? There she is, bent over,
nudging her pendulous breasts into her brassiere
which she so artfully hooks behind her.
And you have seen her step from the shower,
the small triangle of black hair dripping
between her legs.
                         But today you have opened
a door you should not have opened, and your father,
without suit and tie, is not your father.
This is nothing like finding condoms or a *Playboy*
in his night table. No. You've seen Poseidon rise
from the sea, trident in hand; you run from the room.
What did you think a god would wear?

Independent Living

If he doesn't press the button to the right
of the bathroom sink by 11:00 AM,
first the concierge calls, and if he doesn't answer,

someone goes up to make sure he's alive,
and because he has to press it every day,
he's bound to forget now and then—

the phone might ring just as he's heading
toward the bathroom, upsetting the routine
that's come to be the only thing he wants.

That and the keys to the car. Women
who want him more than he wants them.
And his balance, he wants that back too.

The heat in the apartment is set as high
as it will go, and still, he's always cold.
If his skin brushes against the door jamb,

he bleeds. Maybe this is why I've come
to fear the distance between the sidewalk
and my jaw, and maybe this is why

I've started to eat spoonfuls of peanut butter
mid-afternoon, craving calories, fat,
anything to cushion the fall. Skin like paper,

porous, this body a container that leaks.
Body of a body that's had *enough already*,
he tells me, but wants and wants and wants.

The Daughters Play King Lear

No one needs it—two sisters have pianos already
      and the third doesn't play. All her life, their mother
            gave each the same amount of whatever she had

to give: three little girls in pinafores, three girls
      with the same allowance, three tuitions,
            three weddings. But there is only one piano.

Crazy with grief, the father decides he is not ready
      to give it up, just as he is not ready to clean out
            his wife's closet. Still, they all play Cordelia—

one brings him food, one takes him to the doctor, one buys
      him new clothes. They are so good they can't believe
            how good they are, until the plot gets boring

and the daughters begin to have strange dreams—a refrigerator
      opens to a grand display of rotting tomatoes, Wüsthof
            knives float in the air, a cat spins around in the dryer.

The daughters stop sleeping, begin to snap at each other.
      The father takes out his hearing aids as they fight
            over who will be Goneril, who Regan.

Fiction

Tell him his memory retells your history,
watch as he spins out of orbit again . . . Quietly
cover his legs with a quilt. Is your sympathy
sacrifice? What does it matter if he's forgotten?

Childhood's for children, and she was his wife, always
elegant (never a hair out of place)—and the
piano recitals, they set her apart from the women
who never were anything other than mothers

mothering. Each year since her death she gets better
and better. But can there be two different women
remembered? Remembering perfume that stayed
in the room when she left. How she left.

The Second Daughter

I'm not the first to bury a mother, nor the first
to care for a grieving father who was supposed to die
first, nor the first to make every decision, who still

does not believe that nothing more could have been done,
who thinks if only she had not said yes, or maybe it was no,
things would have been different. I'm not the first

who never said goodbye, who will never be sure
her mother knew she was dying but who thinks
that mother loved her best of all and has proof:

that moment in the hospital when the nurses tied her
to the bed because she kept trying to get up to pee
even though everyone knew it was the tumor

pressing on her bladder, her bowels, her spine,
the thing deep in her belly that grew with such speed,
wrapped its arms around the vessels carrying her blood,

no way to cut it out. I'm not the first who sometimes goes
days without thinking about her mother until, at a stop light
on the way to work, I look up into the sky and gasp—

not at the loss—at the dishonor. But that day, that moment
when I pushed her shoulders down as gently as I could
and told her she did not have to get up anymore, pretending

I didn't know she was not ready to die, *goddammit*, that word
she used when she was stuck in traffic—she did not use
that word. Instead she said, *Just one more thing*—

she must have known, right? She must have when
she grabbed me, not my sister, by the wrist and said,
I love you I love you I love you I love you and then let go.

Pledge

Otherwise, who will answer for the empty chair,
and what will become of the plant on the table?

Who will steer the boat out of the canal,
wide-eyed and ready to anchor in another language,

who will unlock the door
and feel for the light switch on the wall?

In the blue-grey of daylight
who will wonder at the fog lifting off the bay?

Otherwise, who will say her name,
sing her story in the flagging hours?

To forget is to forget everything:
the piano on the porch, the smell of perfume,

the way she'd reach her arm across the car
as if she could keep you from flying out.

My Voice

Bright yellow paint spills across the page,
and I see goldfinches clustered around the feeder,
want to say it is the age of rapture, my father
will live forever. Why not? The freezer
was broken two hours ago, and I fixed it myself.
The ice is safe. Some days are like this after all:
my own lane at the pool, a new book by my bed,
the ringing in my ear as much a part of me
as a heartbeat. The colors bleed into each other,
a new vocabulary for the deciduous.
The spiders can stay in the basement, gray hairs
on my head. When I can't take a breath big
enough to fill me, I'll open my bird-mouth and sing.

That New

At the market today, I look for Piñata
apples, their soft-blush-yellow. My husband
brought them home last week, made me guess at
the name of this new strain, held one in his hand
like a gift and laughed as I tried all
the names I knew: Gala, Fuji, Honey
Crisp—watched his face for clues—what to call
something new? It's winter, only tawny
hues and frozen ground, but that apple bride
was sweet, and I want to bring it back to him,
that new. When he cut it, the star inside
held seeds of other stars, the way within
a life are all the lives you might live,
each unnamed, until you name it.

About the Author

author photo by Ken Ronkowitz

Susan Rothbard's poetry has appeared in the *The Cortland Review*, *The Literary Review*, *The National Poetry Review*, and *Poet Lore*, among other journals. Her work also has been featured in Ted Kooser's *American Life in Poetry* and on *Verse Daily*. She earned her MFA in creative writing from Fairleigh Dickinson University and a Doctor of Letters from Drew University. A retired teacher of English and creative writing, she lives in New Jersey.

Previous Winners of The Dogfish Head Poetry Prize

2019 D. L. Perlman *Normal They Napalm the Cottonfields*
The Broadkill River Press, Milton, DE

2018 Becky Gould Gibson, *Indelible*
The Broadkill River Press, Milton, DE

2017 Beth Copeland, *Blue Honey*
The Broadkill River Press, Milton, DE

2016 Mary B. Moore, *Flicker*
The Broadkill River Press, Milton, DE

2015 Faith Shearin, *Orpheus, Turning*
The Broadkill River Press, Milton, DE

2014 Lucian Mattison, *Peregrine Nation*
The Broadkill River Press, Milton, DE

2013 Grant Clauser, *Necessary Myths*
The Broadkill River Press, Milton, DE

2012 Tina Raye Dayton, *The Softened Ground*
The Broadkill Press, Milton, DE

2011 Sherry Gage Chappelle, *Salmagundi*
The Broadkill Press, Milton, DE

2010 Amanda Newell, *Fractured Light*
The Broadkill Press, Milton, DE

2009 David P. Kozinski, *Loopholes*
The Broadkill Press, Milton, DE

2008 Linda Blaskey, *Farm*
Bay Oak Publishers, Dover, DE

2007 Anne Agnes Colwell, *Father's Occupation, Mother's Maiden Name*
Bay Oak Publishers, Dover, DE

2006 Scott Whitaker, *Field Recordings*
Bay Oak Publishers, Dover, DE

2005 Michael Blaine, *Murmur*
Bay Oak Publishers, Dover, DE

2004 Emily Lloyd, *The Most Daring of Transplants*
Argonne House Press, Washington, DC

2003 James Keegan *Of Fathers and Sons*
Argonne House Press, Washington, DC

Dogfish Head is the first American craft brewery to focus on culinary-inspired beer recipes outside traditional beer styles and it has done so since the day it opened with the motto "off-centered ales for off-centered people." Since 1995, Dogfish has redefined craft beer and the way people think about beer by brewing with unique ingredients.

Today, Dogfish is among the fastest-growing breweries in the country and has won numerous awards throughout the years. Dogfish Head has grown into a 200+ person company with a restaurant/brewery/distillery in Rehoboth Beach, a beer-themed inn on the harbor in Lewes and a production brewery/distillery in Milton, Delaware.

Dogfish Head currently sells beer in 37 states and the District of Columbia, and is proud to sponsor The Dogfish Head Poetry prize, awarded now for eighteen consecutive years!

if a poet is
anybody,
he is somebody
to whom
things made
matter very little
...
somebody
who is
obsessed
by
Making.

- e.e. cummings

Cape Gazette

BEACH PAPER   CapeGazette.com

17585 Nassau Commons Boulevard, Lewes • 302.645.7700

Other Titles from The Broadkill River Press

Necessary Myths° ISBN 978-1-940120-92-8	**Poetry by Grant Clauser** $14.95
Peregrine Nation° ISBN 978-1-940120-85-0	**Poetry by Lucian Mattison** $15.95
Flicker ° ISBN 978-1-940120-75-1	**Poetry by Mary B. Moore** $16.95
Sounding the Atlantic ISBN 978-0-9826030-1-7	**Poetry by Martin Galvin** $14.95
That Deep & Steady Hum ISBN 978-0-9826030-2-4	**Poetry by Mary Ann Larkin** $14.95
Exile at Sarzanna ISBN 978-0-9826030-5-5	**Poetry by Laura Brylawski-Miller** $12.00
The Year of the Dog Throwers ISBN 978-0-9826030-3-1	**Poetry by Sid Gold** $12.00
Domain of the Lower Air* ISBN 978-0-9826030-4-8	**Fiction by Maryanne Khan** $14.95
Speed Enforced by Aircraft† ‡ ISBN 978-0-9826030-6-2	**Poetry by Richard Peabody** $15.95
Dutiful Heart ISBN 978-1-940120-91-1	**Poetry by Joy Gaines-Friedler** $16.00
Postcard from Bologna* ISBN 978-1-940-120-90-4	**Poetry by Howard Gofreed** $15.95
Lemon Light ISBN 978-1-940120-94-2	**Poetry by H. A. Maxson** $15.95
On Gannon Street ISBN 978-1-940120-86-7	**Poetry by Mary Ann Larkin** $12.00
The Table of the Elements† ISBN 978-1-940120-93-5	**Poetry by J. T. Whitehead** $15.95
Good with Oranges † ISBN 978-1-940120-83-6	**Poetry by Sid Gold** $16.00
Rock Taught * ISBN 978-1-940120-88-1	**Poetry by David McAleavey** $16.95
Noise ISBN 978-1-940120-70-6	**Poetry by W. M. Rivera** $16.95
Contents Under Pressure † ISBN 978-1-940120-82-9	**Fiction by Ellen Prentiss Campbell** $16.95

* National Book Critics Circle Award Nominee
† National Book Award Nominee
‡ Pulitzer Prize Nominee
° Dogfish Head Poetry Prize Winner

www.ingramcontent.com/pod-product-compliance
Lightning Source LLC
Chambersburg PA
CBHW020216090426

42734CB00008B/1098